John Wesley Powell

John Wesley Powell

D. M. Souza

Franklin Watts
A Division of Scholastic Inc.
New York • Toronto • London • Auckland • Sydney
Mexico City • New Delhi • Hong Kong
Danbury, Connecticut

Note to readers: Definitions for words in **bold** can be found in the Glossary at the back of this book.

Photographs © 2004: Art Resource, NY: 20, 21 (Museum of the City of New York, NY, NY, USA/Scala), 2 (National Portrait Gallery, Smithsonian Institution, Washington, DC, USA); Brown Brothers/U.S. Geological Survey: 39; Corbis Images: 6, 7 (Bettmann), 27 (D. Robert & Lorri Franz), 42 (David Muench), 5, 14, 15, 40 (Scott T. Smith), 34; Grand Canyon National Park: 13 (17226), 49 (17231), 30 (17241), 29 (17254), 5 (GRCA 14765), 44 (GRCA 14765), 43 (GRCA20819); Illinois State University/Transactions of the Illinois State Agricultural Society, Vol. 4, 1859-60: 12; Illinois Wesleyan University, Bloomington, IL/Tate Archives & Special Collections, The Ames Library: 16; John Wesley Powell Museum/Memorial Museum Photo Collection, Page, AZ: 26; National Geographic Image Collection: 38, 50 (Bruce Dale), 22, 23 (Walter Edwards); North Wind Picture Archives: 31, 33; State Historical Society of Iowa, Des Moines/Redhead Family Collection: 18; Superstock, Inc./Newberry Library, Chicago: 46; United States Geological Survey: 37 (J.K. Hillers), 48; Utah State Historical Society: 28; Wisconsin Historical Society/H.H. Bennett Collection, (Whi-4757): 10.

Cover illustration by Stephen Marchesi.
Map by XNR Productions Inc.

The illustration on the cover shows John Wesley Powell. The photograph opposite the title page shows a portrait of Powell by the artist Edmund Clarence Messer, done in 1889.

Library of Congress Cataloging-in-Publication Data

Souza, D. M. (Dorothy M.)
    John Wesley Powell / by D. M. Souza.
        p. cm. — (Watts library)
    Summary: Discusses the life and work of John Wesley Powell, an American geologist and anthropologist who explored the Colorado and Green Rivers.
    Includes bibliographical references (p.) and index.
    ISBN 0-531-12289-1 (lib. bdg.)   0-531-16653-8 (pbk.)
    1. Powell, John Wesley, 1834–1902—Juvenile literature. 2. Explorers—West (U.S.)—Biography—Juvenile literature. 3. Colorado River (Colo.–Mexico)—Discovery and exploration—Juvenile literature. 4. West (U.S.)—Discovery and exploration—Juvenile literature. 5. Soldiers—United States—Biography—Juvenile literature. 6. Scientists—United States—Biography—Juvenile literature. [1. Powell, John Wesley, 1834–1902. 2. Explorers. 3. Geologists. 4. Scientists. 5. Colorado River (Colo.–Mexico)—Discovery and exploration. 6. Grand Canyon (Ariz.)—Discovery and exploration. 7. West (U.S.)—Discovery and exploration.] I. Title. II. Series.
F788 .P88S68 2003
917.91'3044'092—dc22

2003013346

New York Harbor
was often crowded
with ships bringing
immigrants from
England and
European countries.

Chapter One

Early Influences

It was an exciting moment when Joseph Powell, a Methodist minister, his wife Mary, and their two daughters set sail from England in 1830. The Welsh **immigrants** were eager to share in all that the United States had to offer. In their new land, they hoped to raise their children according to Methodist beliefs and to plant the seeds of their faith through Joseph's preaching. The couple soon discovered, however, many forces that made reaching their goals difficult.

When a son was born on March 24, 1834, in Mount Morris, New York, the Powells named him John Wesley, after one of the founders of their religion. They looked forward to training and molding him into a strong spiritual leader just as his namesake had been. What they did not foresee were the many influences that would pull him in other directions.

Eventually John Wesley Powell became a strong **abolitionist**, a student of nature, and a defender of Indian rights and would devote much of his time and energies to the preservation of American Indian cultures. Long before the term "environmentalist" became popular, Powell also struggled to preserve the nation's natural resources for future generations.

"Big George"

John Wesley was only four years old when his family moved to a farming community in Jackson, Ohio. Wes, as he was called, was homeschooled with his brothers and sisters. After lessons, he explored nearby creeks and waterways. It was on one of these outings that he met "Big George" Crookham, a man who left an impression on Wes.

George Crookham, sixty years old and weighing 350

Namesake

John Wesley, an English religious leader, became the head of his brother Charles's Methodist society at Oxford in 1729. In 1735, the brothers traveled to the colony of Georgia as missionaries to convert colonists and American Indians to their religion.

pounds (158 kilograms), read widely, had a keen mind, and loved the outdoors. He despised slavery and regularly aided runaways. In a two-room log cabin on his farm, he set up a classroom filled with stuffed birds, snake skins, rocks, and Indian artifacts, and taught pupils free of charge. Wes became one of Big George's students and from him learned to love reading, exploring nature, and collecting items from nature.

Like Crookham, the Powells opposed slavery and, like him, soon became targets of their pro-slavery neighbors, who vandalized their property and harassed them. The children were ridiculed and pelted with rocks. When the family could no longer risk threats to their lives, they moved to the territory of southern Wisconsin.

Young Farmer

In their new home, the elder Powell traveled the countryside preaching, while Wes and his brother Bram took charge of farming their land. Inexperienced, the boys found the work hard, but it made them physically strong. Although he missed attending school, Wes read during every free moment he had.

One day while working in the fields, he came on the first Indians he had ever met. A group of Winnebago were camping by the creek that ran through the family's property and looked, as he later recalled, "footsore and disconsolate." He learned that the land that his family's farm was on had once been theirs, but government officials pressured them to vacate in exchange for a small payment. Wes was so moved by

Underground Railroad

A network of safe hiding places for thousands of runaway slaves traveling to freedom was active from 1830 to 1860. Crookham was part of this network known as the Underground Railroad.

Powell's encounter with a group of Winnebago Indians made a lasting impression on him.

their story that he later began a lifelong study of American Indian culture.

In the fall of 1850, Wes announced that he was leaving home to continue his education. Not receiving any financial help from his family, he walked 20 miles (32 kilometers) to the closest secondary school. On the outskirts of town, he stopped at a farm where he worked for two weeks to earn the needed funds. The owner was so impressed with the young man that he offered him room and board during the school year in exchange for his continued help on the farm.

From Teacher to War Hero

In the summer, Powell returned home to help his family, but spent as much time as he could studying to become a teacher. When he was only eighteen years old, he was placed in charge of a one-room schoolhouse in Wisconsin. His salary was $14 a month. Some of his pupils were older than he, and he struggled to keep ahead of them in his lessons.

During the next few years, Powell attended various colleges, continued teaching, and, in time, became a principal of a school in Hennepin, Illinois. Summers he spent exploring the countryside. Once, he took a flat-bottomed **skiff** from Minnesota to Louisiana, and camped at night along the shore. Another time, he explored parts of Wisconsin and Michigan on foot. Fascinated by rivers, he also followed the Ohio and Missouri Rivers. During all of these outings, he collected objects from nature and stored thousands of them in his parents' home.

When the Natural History Society of Illinois was formed in June 1858, Powell joined and donated his vast collection to the organization. His specimens were identified and displayed in a museum at the State Normal University, where students were trained to become teachers. Soon his reputation as a **naturalist** spread.

Reservations

During this period, eastern American Indians were often forced from their lands and moved onto **reservations**, large blocks of land, in what was called Indian Territory (present-day Oklahoma). Men, women, and children were sometimes forced to march hundreds of miles even in winter and many died along the way.

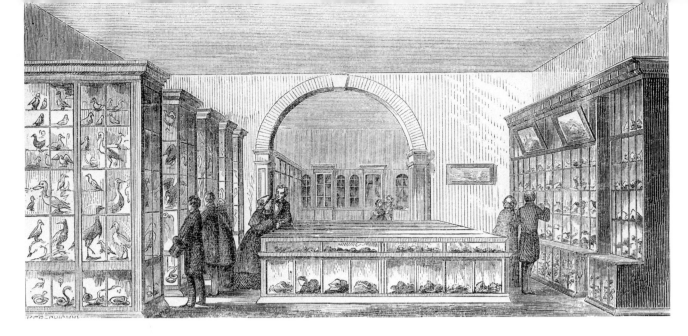

The Museum of Illinois Natural History Society featured many specimens collected by Powell.

The election of Abraham Lincoln in 1860 as president split the states. Although Lincoln won a landslide victory in the North, the Southern states, fearing that he would end slavery, refused to vote for him. A few weeks after his inauguration, South Carolina **seceded** from the Union. By February 1861, six more states followed suit. In the spring, Lincoln called for volunteers to help put down the rebellion.

John Wesley Powell was among the tens of thousands who answered the call. He was immediately appointed as sergeant major of his regiment and was sent to help fortify an area near St. Louis, Missouri. In November, he asked his superior, Brigadier General Ulysses S. Grant, for a short leave to marry Emma Dean, his half cousin. Permission was granted, and after the wedding, Emma returned with him to camp.

Soon, Powell was promoted to captain and moved to the front line. In the fierce battle of Shiloh in April 1862, he was hit in the right wrist by a **musket** ball. His bones were so badly smashed that his arm had to be amputated below the elbow. After recuperating, he returned to active duty and served in several campaigns, eventually being promoted to major. In a letter to a friend, Powell expressed his motives for fighting in the war. "It was a great thing to destroy slavery, but the integrity of the Union was of no less importance. . . ."

In January 1865, at the end of his enlistment term, Powell was discharged from the army. The war continued for four more months, but he and Emma returned to the North, where he began the long process of learning to write and do everything with his left hand. For the rest of his life, he would be reminded daily of the price he had paid for his country.

This photograph shows John W. Powell (right) with his brother William who also fought in the Civil War.

The Battle of Shiloh

This was one of the deadliest battles in the history of modern warfare. Twenty thousand men were killed or wounded in one day.

Powell was intrigued by the American Southwest and hoped to learn more about its lands and peoples.

Chapter Two

Call of the West

The Civil War interrupted the westward growth of the nation, but after the conflict, politicians and businessmen again began promoting expansion. Although much of the wilderness had been mapped, there were still places that were unknown except to American Indians and a handful of fur trappers. The territory stretching across southern Utah and into Arizona was largely unexplored, and maps labeled the area "uncertain." John Wesley Powell was anxious to change this.

University Professor

In the fall of 1865, the war hero became a professor of science at Illinois Wesleyan University in Bloomington. Teaching was just what he needed to lift his spirits again. Like his former instructor, George Crookham, he began taking his students outdoors to experience nature firsthand.

After a year and a half at Illinois Wesleyan University, Powell transferred to Illinois State Normal University. This was the headquarters of the Natural History Society and the museum to which he had contributed his numerous specimens. He was appointed its **curator**, but grew restless for a new challenge. At a board of education meeting, he asked for and received permission to lead an expedition into the Rocky Mountains in order to bring back more specimens.

Powell first had to find a way to finance the journey. The Smithsonian Institution loaned him scientific instru-

This photograph shows the faculty of Illinois Wesleyan University during the 1865–1866 school year. Powell's picture appears in the upper right corner.

ments, and General Grant, then head of the Armies of the United States, provided him with rations at low government rates. After considerable fund-raising, Powell was ready to begin exploring the great "unknown."

Giant Field Trip

In late May 1867, Powell and his wife Emma arrived at Council Bluff, Iowa, where they purchased wagons, horses, mules, and camping equipment. Ten others, including friends, college students, and Powell's brother-in-law, Almon Thompson, eventually joined them. From Council Bluff, the party headed across the plains.

Indians, upset by the increasing number of whites in the area, were terrifying travelers in the region. Powell's party realized this only too well as they passed abandoned wagons, newly dug graves, and deserted houses along the way. To protect themselves, each member of the expedition carried a repeating rifle and a heavy revolver.

In forty days, the party arrived in Denver. From there, they made their way across a treacherous mountain route and climbed Pike's Peak and Mount Lincoln on the **Continental**

Divide. By then, their wagons were loaded with plants, insects, birds, snakes, and various small mammals they had collected along the way.

In September, some members of the expedition returned east, but for another two months, John Wesley Powell and Emma stayed behind and continued their work. They explored the area around the **tributaries** of the Colorado River. Professor Powell gave lectures to the townspeople in Denver and became somewhat of a celebrity. At Hot Sulphur

Springs, he met Jack Sumner, a trader, mountain man, and guide who would later become a member of Powell's expedition.

New Proposal

Returning from his travels in December, Powell met with the board of education to describe the places he had visited, the **flora** and **fauna** collected, and how the funds he was given had been spent. He also let the members know how anxious he was to explore more of the area, especially the Colorado River and the canyons through which it flowed. Everyone was enthusiastic about what he had accomplished and what he was proposing.

The following year, in April 1868, Powell wrote to General Grant telling him of his desire to examine the area. He could,

he maintained, do it for less than it would cost for a military expedition to examine it. He also reminded Grant that it was important to understand this territory inhabited "by powerful tribes of Indians, that will doubtless become hostile as the

prospector and the pioneer encroach upon their hunting ground."

Grant wholeheartedly approved of Powell's plans, and two weeks later, a resolution was introduced in the House of Representatives granting him the right to receive free rations from western military forts. By then, the Union Pacific railroad lines had reached Cheyenne, Wyoming. This meant an exploring party could travel across the plains not by wagon, but by rail. Powell's dream of exploring the last great western wilderness was about to be realized.

Advances in the railroad system enabled Powell's expedition to travel westward much faster than if they had to take wagons.

Powell helped the people of the United States learn more about the mighty Colorado River.

Chapter Three

Down the River

For hundreds of years, little was known of the Colorado River or the Rio Colorado (the red or colored river), as it was called. In 1540, Hernando de Alarcón, a Spanish explorer, was the first European to navigate part of it. He went about 100 miles (160 km) up its course, but was unimpressed and did not explore any further. Another Spaniard, García López de Cárdenas, reached the rim of the Grand Canyon and saw the river below, but was unable to descend into the canyon. In

1776, several Spanish priests reached the Colorado River at a point that later became known as the Crossing of the Fathers.

A few years before the Civil War, Lieutenant Joseph C. Ives attempted to navigate the river. He left in a small paddle-wheel steamer from its mouth at the Gulf of California and went upstream as far as Black Canyon. There, he got stuck on a sand bar and had to continue overland to Diamond Creek. In a report to the government, he expressed his opinion of the area in these words: "Ours has been the first, and will doubt-less be the last, party of whites to visit this profitless locality."

John Wesley Powell's expeditions, however, would paint an entirely different picture. His descriptions of the river and the canyons through which it flowed would in time attract others. Many would arrive simply to witness the beauty of the region.

The Land and its People

On June 29, 1868, Major Powell and his "Colorado River Exploring Expedition" left from the Chicago railway station. In the party were his wife Emma, his brother Walter, Jack Sumner, five students, and various adventure seekers, friends, and war veterans—twenty-one people in all. Many were inexperienced and ill prepared for the hardships of their journey.

In four days, they reached Cheyenne and, after purchasing Mexican ponies, headed 100 miles (160 km) south to Denver. Along the way, the half-wild animals frequently stampeded, and their riders had difficulty both staying mounted and

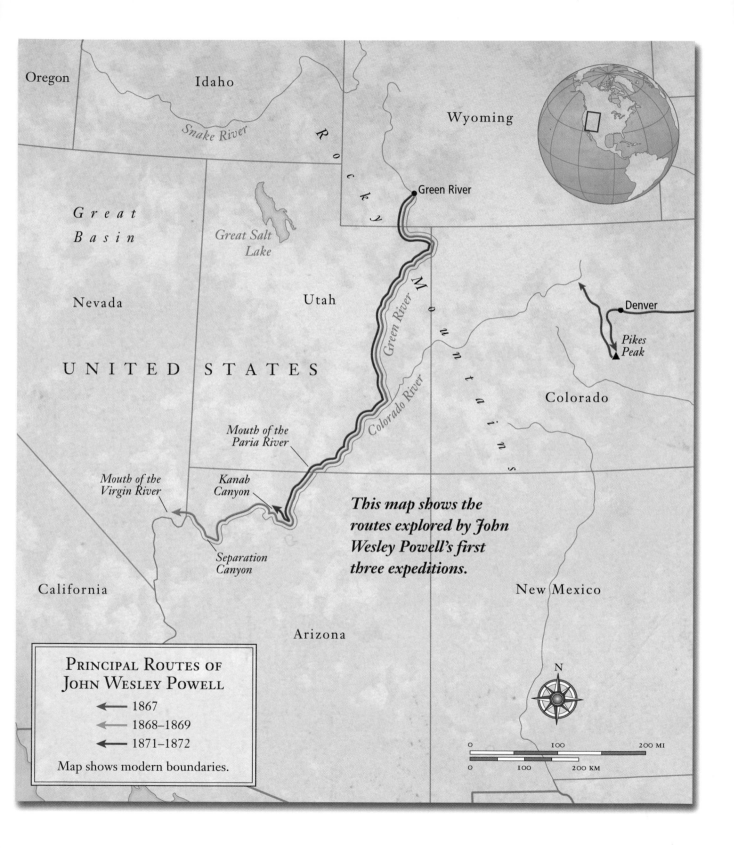

Oregon

Idaho

Snake River

Wyoming

● Green River

Great Basin

Great Salt Lake

Nevada

Utah

● Denver

▲ *Pikes Peak*

Green River

Colorado River

UNITED STATES

Colorado

Mouth of the
Paria River

Mouth of the
Virgin River

Kanab
Canyon

This map shows the
routes explored by John
Wesley Powell's first
three expeditions.

Separation
Canyon

California

New Mexico

Arizona

N

PRINCIPAL ROUTES OF
JOHN WESLEY POWELL

← 1867
← 1868–1869
← 1871–1872

Map shows modern boundaries.

0   100   200 MI
0   100   200 KM

This photograph shows Emma Dean Powell around the time of the expedition.

keeping the ponies from running away. The party carried no tents, and even when it rained, everyone was forced to sleep in the open. In spite of delays, storms, and scarce **game**, they collected numerous wildflowers and other specimens from what one member referred to as "the Great American Desert."

From Denver, they moved on to study the Green River and gather more specimens. A small party, including Powell, his wife, brother Walter, Jack Sumner, and several others, set out to climb the summit of Long's Peak, a 14,000-foot (4,270-meter) mountain that had never been scaled. On the second night, they stopped at the base of Mount McHenry, near present-day Powell Peak. After a grueling climb, they finally reached the top and held a flag-raising ceremony.

On their return, some in the party decided they had had enough of exploring and returned east. Eight others moved with Powell and his wife closer to the mouth of the White River. There they built cabins and spent the winter learning more about the river, the land, and its native population. Powell relished every moment of his experiences with the natural world.

Plans for a River Run

After exploring the area around the Colorado River and its tributaries, talking with hunters and American Indians, Powell felt certain that the river could be navigated in small boats. He returned to Chicago to have four boats specially built. Emma went to Detroit to stay with her family during the coming year.

One of the first challenges Powell encountered on the expedition was climbing Long's Peak.

Friendly Ute Indians

A group of Ute Indians lived close to the Powell encampment. Powell often visited them, studied their language and customs, and also purchased items of clothing, cooking utensils, and ornaments that he later presented to several museums.

The members of the expedition were reunited at Green River Station in Wyoming.

Special Boats

Three of the boats, *Kitty Clyde's Sister*, *No Name*, and *Maid of the Canyon*, measured 21 feet (6.4 m) long, were made of oak, and had watertight compartments at either end. A smaller boat, the *Emma Dean*, was made of pine and had the same type of compartments.

While his vessels were being built, Powell raised the needed funds from several universities and museums. Then he rejoined the nine members of the expedition waiting for him near the Green River Station in Wyoming. The transcontinental railroad now crossed the river and made it possible for his boats to be shipped by rail and unloaded directly from a flatbed car into the water. For two weeks, the men loaded supplies onto the vessels and prepared for the next phase of their adventure.

"We are quite proud of our little fleet as it lies in the river waiting for us to embark," wrote Powell. ". . . the waves rocking the little vessels, and the current of the Green, swollen, mad and seeming eager to bear us down through its mysterious canyons." The boats held enough food for ten months, a large store of ammunition, animal traps, scientific instruments, axes, saws, hammers, and nails.

On May 24, 1869, the men pushed away from shore and moved downriver. Most had fought in the Civil War on the side of the Union. Although they were used to taking orders, they were all fiercely independent.

Major Powell, strapped to a chair, rode in the lead boat with Jack Sumner and William Dunn at the oars. Within a short time, *Kitty Clyde's Sister* grounded on a sand bar, and another boat broke an oar. In spite of these delays, the expedition advanced about 8 miles (13 km) before pulling ashore for the first night of rest.

This photograph, taken on a later expedition, shows the special chair Powell used on his boat.

A Wild Ride

During the next few rainy days, everyone struggled to keep dry and warm. When they weren't riding the currents, some were tramping through mud, searching for **fossils**. Others were hunting sheep, beaver, or whatever else they could find to cook over open campfires.

By June, the men reached the Red Canyon, whose walls towered on either side of them. There the water roared loudly

Powell thought that the rapids in Red Canyon were too dangerous to travel over by boat.

and raced along at "railroad speed." The boats rose and fell as if riding bucking horses. When falls appeared too dangerous, Powell ordered the men to unload the crafts and lower them by lines beyond the **rapids**. At other times, he had them **portage**, or carry, the boats overland.

One evening, the party camped at Browns Hole, or Browns Park, which is now a national wildlife refuge. The next day, the men entered a dark canyon more than 20 miles (32 km) long. Powell named it Lodore, and it turned out to be the scene of several disasters.

At one point, someone in the lead boat signaled the approach of dangerous falls, but crewmen aboard the *No Name* failed to see the warning. They plunged over the falls, were carried over a second set of falls, and crashed into a rock. Their boat split in two, and the men were thrown into the foaming waters. After a desperate rescue, all were brought to safety, but their provisions disappeared.

The next morning, some in the party managed to salvage several pieces of scientific equipment. Lost, however, was a third of their food and clothing supplies. Powell named this place "Disaster Falls."

A little farther downriver, the expedition set up camp and

the cook started a fire to prepare the evening meal. Because of strong winds, the fire quickly became a "sheet of flames." Powell was hiking on the side of the canyon and saw the men rushing into the water with whatever items they could rescue. Lost in this mishap were cooking pans, spoons, plates, cups, a pickax, and a shovel. A few items were later salvaged from the fire, but the men then had to make do with far less equipment.

Soon, the expedition reached the point where the Uinta River flows into the Green River. The party camped, and several men searched for new supplies at a nearby government post. Although much of their remaining food was spoiled, all they managed to find at the post was 300 pounds (135 kg) of flour. Expedition member Frank Goodman, who had been in the boat wreck, decided he was finished with exploring and remained behind.

A fire at the expedition's campsite resulted in the loss of utensils and tools.

Several weeks later, the party entered the Colorado River—wide, deep, and cocoa-colored. The waters were calm for a while, but then changed to rapids. The boats frequently had to be portaged. Those that were battered by rough waters soon sprang leaks and had to be repaired with **pitch** from nearby pine trees.

Next, the party entered what they called Cataract Canyon. Rapids pounded the boats repeatedly. Even when the waters turned calm, some of the men began complaining. They were anxious to complete their journey, but Powell frequently wanted to stop and examine the canyon walls or collect specimens. Hungry and exhausted, some members of the party were at the point of **mutiny**.

Farther on lay the canyon that men had talked about for more than two hundred years—the Grand Canyon. On August 13, Powell made this entry in his journal: "We are three quarters of a mile in the depths of the earth, and the great river shrinks into insignificance as it dashes its angry waves against the walls and cliffs that rise to the world above. . . .We have an unknown distance yet to run, an unknown river to explore. . . ."

By August 27, with food supplies low, the expedition reached the most violent rapids they had yet seen. Three members of the party wanted to search for an overland route and announced that they were leaving. Powell, however, was determined to ride the raging waters. He abandoned the *Emma Dean* and left the scientific equipment and articles they had collected in a safe place along the shore. Six remaining members then lifted the two boats over a line of rocks and successfully ran the foaming waters. Three days later, at the mouth of the Virgin River in Arizona, they reached a settlement established by members of the Mormon Church. They had traveled about 1,000 miles (1,600 km), had not had a decent meal in more than three months, and were exhausted. There they learned that the three party members who had traveled overland had been ambushed and killed by Indians.

Return From the Dead

For months, the story circulated that everyone in the Colorado River Exploring Expedition had perished. When Powell returned to the east, he was quickly hailed as a hero. Audiences packed the halls where Powell lectured. Newspapers and magazines wrote about the adventurers, and everyone was eager to hear more about the places they had explored. Powell, however, could not wait to return to the Colorado area.

Powell and his expedition struggled in the rough waters of the Grand Canyon.

Not only was it important to explore the West, but the U.S. government also wanted people to survey the land so that maps could be made of the region.

Chapter Four

Surveying the Plateau

Once western lands were discovered and explored, leaders in Washington, D.C., wanted to know more about them and their value to the nation. Each area had to be **surveyed**. Rivers, lakes, and mountains had to be carefully mapped, and their bones, fossils, rocks, and minerals cataloged.

Before the Civil War, the Army's Corps of **Topographical** Engineers had done most of the survey work. Later, a group of civilian surveyors entered the

Western Surveyors

The best known of the western surveyors of the period were Ferdinand Vandiveer Hayden, Clarence King, and George M. Wheeler.

field. Powell realized that to continue doing the work he loved, he would have to organize a survey party.

During the winter of 1869–1870, Powell lived in Normal, Illinois, and spent his time lecturing, working as curator, and searching for friendly politicians in Washington, D.C., who would help fund a survey. With a letter of support from the secretary of the Smithsonian Institution, he finally succeeded in obtaining a $12,000 grant from Congress in July 1870. This allowed him to hire a small staff and begin making plans for what became officially known as the Geographical and Geological Survey of the Rocky Mountain Region.

Groundwork

Powell was determined to travel the Green and the Colorado Rivers without the mishaps of the first journey. For several months, he searched for overland routes where food and other supplies could be brought to members of the expedition. He also wished to establish peaceful relations with the various Indian groups living in the area. Although he had become friendly with the Ute, he wanted to reach out to others.

Joseph Hamblin, a Mormon scout who lived in the plateau and canyon country, had considerable contact with Indians. One day, Powell met with him and asked for his assistance. Hamblin agreed to set up a meeting with the Kaibab, Uinkaret, and Shivwit, local bands of Paiute who lived along the North Rim of the Grand Canyon. In September, everyone came together at the Place of Pines.

Powell was fascinated by what he saw and showed genuine interest in the customs of the people. They called him "Kapu-rats" or One-Arm-Off. By the time he and Hamblin left the encampment, Powell had increased his Indian vocabulary and had filled his packs with baskets, items of clothing, and tribal ornaments, all destined for the Smithsonian Institution. He had shown respect for the Indians and in turn had won their respect.

John Wesley Powell (right) talks with a member of the Paiute tribe.

A New Experience

In May 1871, Powell and ten members of the Geographical and Geological Survey met in Green River City, Wyoming. No one was a trained scientist. Instead, Powell chose friends, relatives, war veterans, and farmers. Almon H. Thompson, Powell's brother-in-law and a superintendent of schools in Bloomington, Illinois, would become

This photograph of Powell's encampment on the Green River in 1871 was taken by E. O. Beaman.

the group's surveyor. John F. Steward, a farmer and friend of Powell, would act as geologist.

Other surveyors often took along distinguished photographers and artists. Wishing to do the same, Powell hired E. O. Beaman as photographer and Clem Powell, his cousin, as assistant. Eighteen-year-old Frederick Dellenbaugh signed on as artist. The other men in the group served as boatmen, assistants, or cooks.

The men spent three weeks making preparations and packing new boats. The *Emma Dean*, the *Nellie Powell*, and the *Canonita* were similar to the larger boats used on the first trip. On May 22, the expedition moved downriver with Powell again strapped to a chair in the lead boat. Jack Sumner, the mountain man, had agreed to join them, but was unable to make it because of snows high up in the mountains where he was trapping furs. To replace him, Powell hired a German immigrant named Jack Hillers.

The river did not fascinate Powell as much as it had on the first expedition. He was more interested in learning about the surrounding land and the Indians living in the area. For this reason, he frequently left the group to visit the tribes and explore the canyons and **plateaus**, some of which became part of Zion National Park. During his absence, his brother-in-law took charge and enforced a daily schedule to keep the men busy and out of fights.

By the end of August, Powell returned bringing with him a small supply of flour, meat, and sugar. Back in his chair, he led

Photography

Photographers at the time made use of a technique known as wet-plate photography. Pieces of glass were coated with chemicals and then placed in a large camera. Once a picture was taken, it had to be developed immediately in a dark tent. To get the best pictures, this bulky equipment was often carried up and down steep cliffs.

On his second expedition, Powell spent more time learning about the native peoples who lived in the region.

the party down rough stretches of the river and finally reached the mouth of the Dirty Devil. There, he decided to leave the *Canonita*, half filled with photographic chemicals, in a cave until spring. Ten men in two boats raced through Glen Canyon and past the mouth of the San Juan River. At the Crossing of the Fathers, a shipment of supplies was waiting for them. The weary men welcomed the sight of food, magazines, clothing, and mail.

It was then October and winter was fast approaching. Powell announced that the party would spend the winter at a Mormon settlement known as Kanab. When summer arrived, they would run the river through the Grand Canyon.

The Canyon Run

The following year, while Powell went to Washington, D.C., to raise additional funds, Thompson again resumed command of the group. The men mapped much of the land of the Grand Canyon. They explored the Henry, an unknown mountain range, and discovered a river they named the Escalante. Several in the party resigned, among them Beaman, the photographer, but Jack Hillers took his place.

In August, Powell returned and was anxious to travel the Colorado River through the Grand Canyon. But miners had discovered the boats hidden along the shore and had stolen the supplies. Two vessels were eventually salvaged and equipped for the journey.

As the group roared through Marble Canyon, the boats were battered by waves and began leaking. Rain fell for several days, soaking the men, their rations, blankets, and guns. Three days later, the river was much higher than it had been on the first expedition. Waves crashed against rocks, sending sprays 30 feet (9 m) into the air. At one point, the *Emma Dean* hit a rapid and was quickly swamped. Crew and supplies spilled into the water, and Powell and Hillers were sucked into a whirlpool. They were rescued, but a new problem arose.

Published Works

A Canyon Voyage by Fred Dellenbaugh was published in 1908, and the diary of Almon Thompson in 1939. *Photographed All the Best Scenery*, by Jack Hillers, was not released until 1972.

The Grand Canyon is the deepest gorge of Colorado River.

News arrived that a band of Shivwit Indians was upset about the murder of some of its people. They were threatening revenge on whites. Powell did not wish the disaster of the first expedition to be repeated. He announced that the canyon run would end. The rest of the area could be mapped when the situation with the Indians quieted.

The men could be proud of what they had accomplished. Several had kept diaries of the journey, which were later published. Powell himself wrote an account, *The Canyons of the*

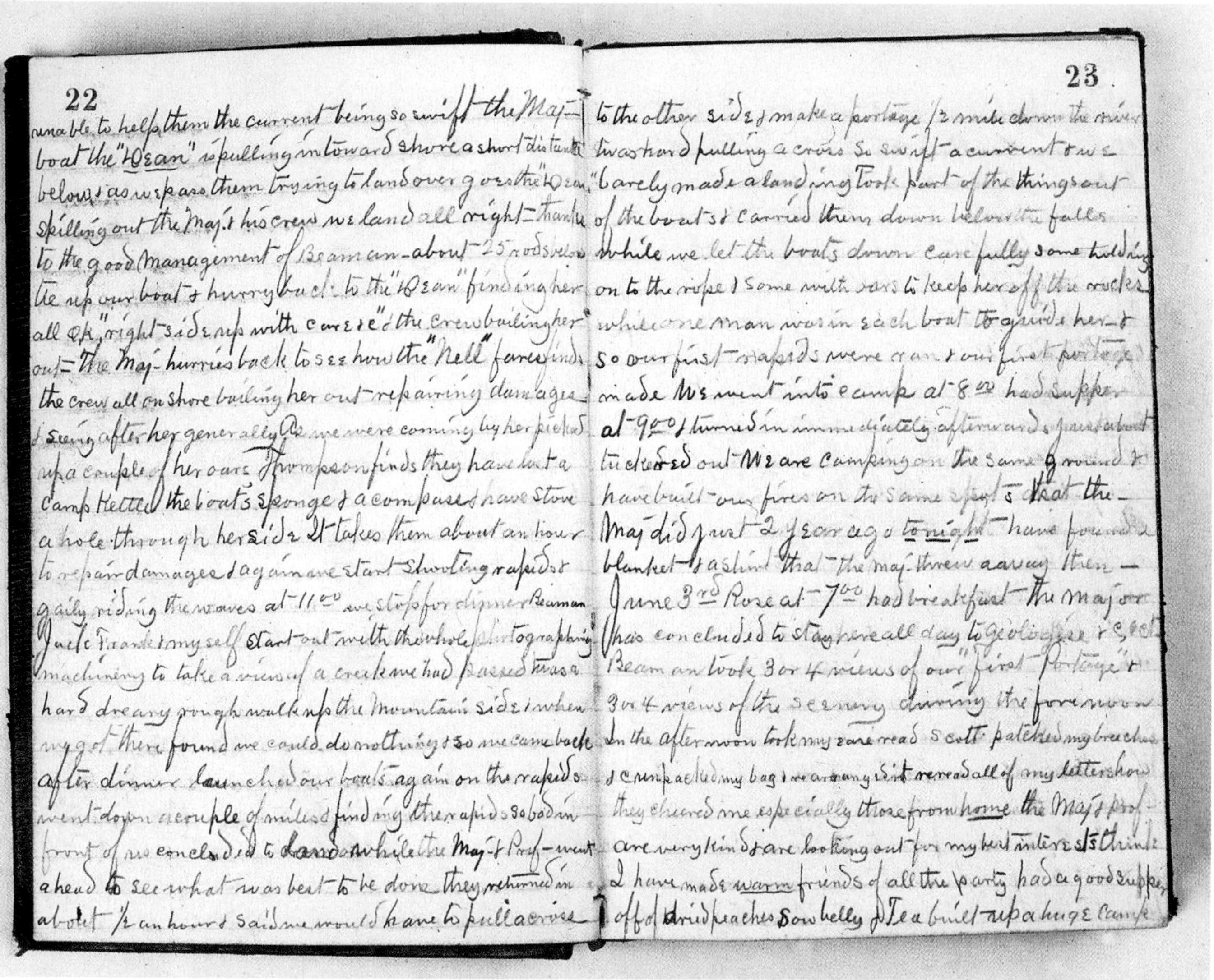
22

unable to help them the current being so swift the Maj—
boat the "Dean" is pulling in toward shore a short distance
below & as we pass them trying to land over goes the "Dean"
spilling out the Maj. & his crew we land all right — thanks
to the good management of Beaman — about 25 rods below
tie up our boat & hurry back to the "Dean" finding her
all O.K. "right side up with care" & the crew bailing her
out — The Maj. hurries back to see how the "Nell" fares finds
the crew all on shore bailing her out repairing damages
& seeing after her generally As we were coming by her picked
up a couple of her oars Thompson finds they have lost a
camp kettle the boat's sponge & a compass & have stove
a hole through her side It takes them about an hour
to repair damages & again we start shooting rapids &
gaily riding the waves at 11.00 we stop for dinner Beaman
Jack Frank & myself start out with the whole photographing
machinery to take a view of a creek we had passed was a
hard dreary rough walk up the mountain side & when
we got there found we could do nothing & so we came back
after dinner launched our boats again on the rapids
went down a couple of miles & finding the rapids so bad in
front of us concluded to land while the Maj. & Prof. went
ahead to see what was best to be done they returned in
about 1/2 an hour & said we would have to pull across

23

to the other side & make a portage 1/2 mile down the river
was hard pulling across so swift a current & we
barely made a landing took part of the things out
of the boats & carried them down below the falls
while we let the boats down carefully some holding
on to the rope & some with oars to keep her off the rocks
while one man was in each boat to guide her — &
so our first rapids were run & our first portage
made We went into camp at 8.00 had supper
at 9.00 & turned in immediately afterwards just about
tuckered out We are camping on the same ground &
have built our fires on the same spots that the —
Maj. did just 2 years ago tonight have found a
blanket & a shirt that the Maj. threw away then —
June 3rd Rose at 7.00 had breakfast the Major
has concluded to stay here all day to geologize &c &c.
Beaman took 3 or 4 views of our "First Portage" &
3 or 4 views of the scenery during the forenoon
In the afternoon took my ease read Scott patched my breeches
& [illegible] my bag & rearranging it reread all of my letters how
they cheered me especially those from home the Maj & Prof.
are very kind & are looking out for my best interests I think
I have made warm friends of all the party had a good supper
off of dried peaches sow belly & Tea built up a huge camp

This photograph shows the expedition journal of Walter Clement Powell, the nephew of John Wesley Powell.

Colorado, which included events from both expeditions. Hundreds of photographs were taken of the western lands and its peoples, and these excited the imagination of the public. Powell and the members of both his expeditions had succeeded in lifting the curtain on an area that had once been a mystery.

*Powell (second on the left) takes a break from
exploring southwestern plateaus.*

Chapter Five

A Changing Nation

When the second trip down the Colorado River was halted in September 1872, Powell's career did not end. He continued exploring and studying native tribes in the area he called the "Plateau Province," which included eastern and southern Utah, western Colorado, northern Arizona, and parts of northern New Mexico. During the next several years, his men completed the mapping of the Grand Canyon and added to their

Powell was concerned about how the western lands were being settled.

collections by photographing not only the landscape of the region, but its people.

Powell became convinced that management of western lands was vital to the future success of the nation. Eighty years earlier, with the Land Ordinance of 1785, Thomas Jefferson had divided the lands north of the Ohio River and east the Mississippi River into checkerboard plots suitable for small, independent farms. Each parcel was level, sometimes wooded, and relatively equal in value.

In 1862, to attract settlers to lands west of the Mississippi, Congress passed the Homestead Act. It gave anyone twenty-one years of age or older who was willing to settle on and work a plot of land for five years the right to own that land. Powell knew that western lands could not be divided or distributed in this way. Mountains, deserts, and limited water supplies made much of the area useless for agriculture.

Instead, he believed that developments should be centered around **watersheds**, or regions drained by rivers or streams. He fought long and hard to change the federal system of land management in the western lands. Powerful interests, however, opposed his ideas and defeated them.

The Study of American Indians

Powell believed that "strict justice and the widest charity" should be extended to the native peoples of the western regions. He did not see them as savages, as many others did, but as human beings deserving of respect. He repeatedly listened to them tell about the hardships of losing lands they had lived on for hundreds of years, about losing rights to rivers, streams, and forests that were the source of their livelihood. He saw how rapidly their way of life was coming to an end.

In an effort to help the public better understand and appreciate the American Indians, Powell organized the Bureau of Ethnology as part of the Smithsonian Institution. Its purpose was to undertake a massive study of the languages and the "customs, laws, governments, institutions, mythologies, religions and even arts" of diverse Indian tribes. The work of the bureau became an important part of his life. A five-volume report, *Handbook of American Indians*, published

Special Friend

Chuarumpeak ("Chuar") was one of the leaders of the Kaibab Indians who became a longtime friend of Powell and told him the legends of the Paiute.

At the Smithsonian Institution, Powell studied American Indian cultures.

after his death, was the result of the bureau's findings. It was the most complete examination of American Indians that had yet been done.

Powell believed that Indians, like whites, wanted the same things—peace, stability, the means of making a livelihood, and the chance to improve themselves. He felt that they could achieve these things while living on reservations if the government carefully maintained them. Eventually, however, he looked forward to the day when Indians could become a vital part of white society.

Land Management

The years following Powell's expeditions were marked by rapid economic development. People were searching for land, money, and a way to make a fortune. The southern part of the nation—Oklahoma, New Mexico, Arizona, and Utah—did not yet enjoy statehood, and the nation wanted to know how these areas could best be developed.

Powell's *Report on the Lands of the Arid Region of the United States*, released in 1878, proposed that water was the key to success in this area. In some places, it could be diverted from rivers and streams to **irrigate** crops. Places without water, he proposed, should be used for forests, cattle grazing, or left alone. Government surveys could determine which areas could be irrigated.

Industry, developers, and settlers eager for land all opposed Powell's proposals, which in the end were defeated. In time, however, his report was recognized as one of the most important written on the management of land. Today, with water supplies dwindling, Powell's argument for limited development in arid regions seems more important than ever.

Powell was successful in convincing Congress that his survey work and that of Wheeler, Hayden, and King should be combined into one set of maps. The creation of the U.S. Geological Survey was the result, and King became its first director. A year later, Powell succeeded him and remained in office until 1894.

Powell worked tirelessly throughout his life for the cause of science. He helped found the Cosmos Club, a group that established the National Geographic Society in 1888. He was a member of the National Academy of Sciences, and for a time was president of the American Association for the Advancement of Science.

Powell wrote a report encouraging the U.S. government and its people to consider the importance of water in settling the West.

After a period of declining health, Powell died at his family's cottage in Brooklin, Maine, on September 23, 1902. The Civil War hero, who learned as a young boy the excitement of exploring nature, was buried in Arlington National Cemetery. On his tombstone are the words "Soldier. Explorer. Scientist."

John Wesley Powell willed his brain to science at his death. His preserved brain is a part of the collection of the National Museum of Natural History.

A STUDY OF THE BRAIN OF THE LATE MAJOR J. W. POWELL
By EDWARD ANTHONY SPITZKA

INTRODUCTION

The fortunate preservation of the brain of Major J. W. Powell affords another opportunity for placing on record the cerebral characteristics of a distinguished man. Major Powell will ever be remembered for the vigorous brainy qualities by means of which he exerted a great influence upon his fellow-workers and greatly favored the progress of those branches of science to which he was so devoted. His personality was one which will remain clear in the memory of all who knew him; the forceful energy which earned him the leading position in the ranks of those who have his clear foresight, his courage, energy...

Timeline

1834	John Wesley Powell is born in Mount Morris, New York, on March 24.
1838	The Powell family moves from New York to Ohio.
1846	The Powell family moves from Ohio to the territory of Wisconsin.
1852	Powell begins teaching in Wisconsin.
1860	Powell becomes a principal of a school in Hennepin, Illinois.
1861	Powell enlists in the Illinois Infantry in the spring and marries Emma Dean in November.
1862	Powell is wounded at the Battle of Shiloh and loses part of his right arm.
1865	Powell is discharged from the army.
1867	Powell leads an expedition to the Rocky Mountains.
1868–1869	The expedition travels down the Colorado River and explores the area.
1871–1872	Powell conducts an official survey of the Rocky Mountains.
1878	The report *The Lands of the Arid Regions of the United States* is published.
1879–1902	Powell becomes director of the Bureau of Ethnology of the Smithsonian Institution.
1881–1894	Powell is named director of the U.S. Geological Survey.
1888	As a member of the Cosmos Club, Powell helps found the National Geographic Society.
1902	Powell dies on September 23 in the Haven Colony of Brooklin, Maine.

Glossary

abolitionist—a person who struggled to end the practice of slavery

Continental Divide—a ridge of high ground through the Rocky Mountains that separates waters flowing westward from those flowing eastward

curator—a person in charge of a museum

fauna—animals of a particular region

flora—plants of a particular region

fossil—a preserved remain or trace of a living animal or plant

game—wild animals hunted for food, sport, or profit

immigrant—a person who moves to another country

irrigate—to supply water to crops by diverting it from rivers or streams

kiva—a chamber in which religious ceremonies were practiced by Anasazi Indians

musket—a type of gun similar to the modern-day rifle

mutiny—a rebellion of soldiers or seamen against their leader

naturalist—a person who studies plants and animals

pitch—sap found in the bark of pine trees

plateau—a high, flat land that has steep slopes on at least one side

portage—to carry a boat or goods overland

rapids—an often rocky part of a river where water runs very swiftly

reservation—a tract of land set aside by the U.S. government for use by American Indians

seceded—withdrew

skiff—a small, one-person boat

survey—to examine the boundaries of an area and study its natural resources

tributary—a stream or river that flows into a larger body of water

topographical—relating to topography, the detailed description of a region determined by means of a survey

watershed—a region drained by a river or a stream

To Find Out More

Books

Alter, Judy. *Exploring and Mapping the American West*. Danbury, CT: Children's Press, 2001.

Arnold, James, Roberta Wiener. *Divided in Two: The Road to Civil War, 1861*. Minneapolis, MN: Lerner Publications, 2002.

Bruns, Roger. *John Wesley Powell: Explorer of the Grand Canyon*. New Jersey: Enslow Publishers, 1997.

Maurer, Richard, *The Wild Colorado: The True Adventures of Fred Dellenbaugh*. New York: Crown Books, 1999.

Nardo, Don. *The Indian Wars: From Frontier to Reservation*. San Diego, CA: Lucent Books, 2001.

Rawlins, Carol B. *The Colorado River*. Danbury, CT: Franklin Watts, 1999.

Santella, Andrew. *Mountain Men*. Danbury, CT: Children's Press, 2003.

Videos and Films

Grand Canyon: Symphony of Stone. Panorama International Productions, 2000.

Lost in the Grand Canyon. PBS, 1998.

River of Stone: The Powell Expedition. Libraryvideo.com, 1997.

Rivers of North America: The Colorado. Film Ideas, 2001.

The Trail of Tears. Films for the Humanities, 2000.

Organizations and Online Sites

Eiteljorg Museum of American Indians and Western Art
500 West Washington St.
Indianapolis, IN 46204
http://www.eiteljorg.org/index2.html
Through art works and artifacts, this museum highlights the history and cultures of the American Indians. It also reveals something of the lifestyles of present-day Native Americans.

Images of Glen Canyon
http://glencanyon.org/facts/penningtonphotos.htm
On this site, you can take a virtual tour through the Glen Canyon.

John Wesley Powell Memorial Museum
#6 N. Lake Powell Blvd.
Page, AZ 86040
http://powellmuseum.org
This museum features sketches, photos, and a replica of one of the boats used by Powell on his Colorado River expedition. It also has a collection of American Indian artifacts.

John Wesley Powell River History Museum
885 E. Main St.
Green River, UT 84525
http://www.surweb.org/surweb/tour/jwp/jwprhm.htm
Here you will find photos, artifacts, displays, and maps describing the two expeditions of the Green and Colorado Rivers, as well as information on the history of the rivers.

The Smithsonian Institution
1000 Jefferson Dr. S.W.
Washington, D.C. 20013
http://www.si.edu/museums/
This Institution is made up of fourteen museums, the National Zoo in Washington, D.C., and two museums in New

York City, one of which is the American Indian Museum. All contain displays and artifacts designed to increase the visitor's knowledge of history, culture, and science. The institution's website has numerous topics for students to explore.

The United States Geological Survey
511 National Center
Reston, Virginia 20192
http://www.usgs.gov/education/
This government organization attempts to manage our natural resources and help us understand the Earth around us. Its *Learning Web* is filled with information about the natural world.

A Note on Sources

Exploring the Grand Canyon gave me a better idea of the awesome feeling Powell and his companions must have experienced when they first saw the area. Reading Powell's book, *The Canyons of the Colorado*, gave hints of his thoughts and impressions during the first and second expeditions. The field notes and diaries of Almon Thompson, Fred Dellenbaugh, and Jack Hillers made clear the day to day hardships suffered by those on the second expedition.

Two volumes were helpful in revealing Powell's ideas on the West and on Native American Indians—*Report on the Lands of the Arid Region of the United States*, and *Manuscripts on the Numic Peoples of Western North America*. Two other books about the explorer and about his life—*Beyond the Hundredth Meridian* by Wallace Stegner, and *A River Running West* by Donald Worster, filled in important details about the man and his life. Another book by Steven Carothers, *The Colorado River Through Grand Canyon: Natural History and Human Change*, made clear the importance of the river to the entire Southwest.

—*D. M. Souza*

Index

Numbers in *italics* indicate illustrations.

About the Author

After teaching in both middle grades and high school for several years, D. M. Souza began writing. She has written more than two dozen books on science and nature for young people. In her free time, she enjoys exploring wilderness areas and learning about wild animals. One of the most enjoyable parts of writing about explorers for Franklin Watts was being able to retrace some of the paths they took through unexplored territories.